The Power of a Prophetic Mindset Workbook

© Copyright 2016 – Cynthia Thompson

All rights reserved. No part of this book may be reproduced, stored in a retrieval system, or transmitted in any form or by any means- electronic, mechanical, photocopying, recording, or otherwise, without prior written permission of the copyright owner, except by a reviewer who wishes to quote brief passages in connection with a review for inclusion in a magazine, newspaper, or broadcast.

Biblical scripture quotations are taken from King James, NIV, The Message and Amplified bible, unless otherwise stated. All emphasis within Scripture quotations is the author's own.

International Standard Book Number:

978-0-9894680-5-3

Design by Shaquille Coleby

FOR SPEAKING ENGAGEMENTS AND MORE INFORMATION ABOUT ETERNAL CHANGE MINISTRIES

AND THE PROPHETIC TRAINING CENTER CALL:
(954) 531-6269

EMAIL: **prophetcynthia@prophetictrainingcenter.com**

WEBSITE: **www.eternalchangeministries.org**

Published by **Divine Works Publishing**
Wellington, Florida 33414 (561) 247-1359

info@divineworkspublishing.com

INDEX

Objectives 1

Introduction 2

Chapter 1   The Human Mind 4

Chapter 2   Transformation of the Mind 6

Chapter 3   Understanding the Prophetic 9

Chapter 4   Cultivating a Prophetic Mindset 12

Chapter 5   A Higher Way of Thinking 14

Chapter 6   The Prophetic Spirit 17

Chapter 7   The Mind of Prophecy 20

Chapter 8   Prophetic Prayer 22

Answers 24

Notes 32

Bibliography 37

OBJECTIVES

1. To comprehend the mind of God.

2. To understand how to access and operate in the power of the prophetic in our daily lives.

3. To practically apply the principles learned through this course to construct the full prophetic purpose not only for your life but for everyone who you are called to impact in ministry and the global marketplace.

INTRODUCTION

Most people automatically relegate the prophetic to the church or to the prophet and prophetic ministry, but the prophetic has been in existence since the foundation of the worlds. Contrary to popular belief, the prophetic is not just prophecy; it is the ministry of spiritual interpretation and it involves everyone who is willing to shift and tap into accessing God's mind. God desires for everyone to know and understand the prophetic, because it is how He operates in people, places and things to manifest and accomplish His will in the earth.

We are living in a prophetic time where God declared, "In the last days, I will pour out my Spirit upon all people. Your sons and daughters will prophesy. Your young men will see visions, and your old men will dream dreams." As people all over the world are overcome with fear due to terror and gross darkness upon the land, it has become critical to know the mind of God so that we have the advantage to remain ahead of the curve.

At the end of this course, students will have a greater understanding of how to operate with a prophetic mindset and to be connected to the heartbeat, rhythms and pulse of God.

CHAPTER 1 QUESTIONS
THE HUMAN MIND

For to be carnally minded is death; but to be spiritually minded is life and peace. Because the carnal mind is enmity against God for it is not subject to the law of God, neither indeed can be. **Romans 8:6-7 KJV**

KEY TERMS

Conscious - awake and able to understand what is happening around you
Unconscious - not marked by conscious thought, sensation, or feeling
Subconscious - existing in the part of the mind that a person is not aware of: existing in the mind but not consciously known or felt

The human mind is the faculty of consciousness and thought that enables an individual to process old and new experiences, good and bad thoughts and feelings. The mind influences how we function and operate every day. There are three parts of the mind the conscious, subconscious, and unconscious and all of them work together to create our natural reality.

1. Why does the human mind oppose the mind of God?

2. What are the names of the two types of minds?

3. Which part of the mind stores memories and past experiences?

4. What does God desire for believers to live in?

5. The conscious mind directs your ability to _____ and whatever you focus on, you will _____ become.

6. What is limited to the earth realm?

7. Which sense gives people the ability to perceive the unseen world?

8. How does the unconscious mind function?

9. Complete this phrase:
   Understanding the human mind and how it functions is essential to getting to the _____.

10. How does the conscious mind function?

11. Every _____ is broken when you operate with a prophetic mindset because you see things from Heaven's perspective, which is the mind of God.

12. What attitude permits someone to always be on the top?

CHAPTER 2 QUESTIONS
TRANSFORMATION OF THE MIND

Do not conform to the pattern of this world, but be transformed by the renewing of your mind. Then you will be able to test and approve what God's will is—his good, pleasing and perfect will.

Romans 12:2 NIV

KEY TERMS

Metamorphosis - a major change in the appearance or character of someone or something

Wrestling - to struggle to move, deal with, or control something

Transformation in and of itself means to change completely, which means that whatever the thing is that is being changed has done so to the point of being totally reconfigured and looks nothing like it looked before the metamorphosis occurred. So, in order to transform the mind, there must be a dramatic change in the way one thinks and acts. When the mind is transformed your very character and nature take on a new identity.

1. What is the first thing that must happen in order "test and approve what God's will" is for your life?

2. In order to transform the mind, there must be a dramatic change in the way one _____ and _____, such that the individual is virtually a stranger to his family, friends, and foes.

3. Why does disobedience stop or block transformation?

4. God rules the _____ and he put us here to rule the _____, the only problem with this, is that we cannot rule with a mind that does not think God's thoughts.

5. When the mind is transformed what takes on a new identity?

6. Daily, we must _____ with the thoughts that run through our own minds.

7. There is a mindset that will always _____ the flow of the _____ and this is the _____.

8. What does Eden symbolize from a spiritual perspective?

9. What did Norman Vincent Peele say about the power of a person's thoughts?

10. "Sin thoughts" can be described as?

11. _____ is one of the main opponents you will have to wrestle and take down in order to have a prophetic mindset.

12. God _____ and _____ designed us to win from the foundations of the world.

13. A _____ or _____ mindset will always be at odds with the prophetic mindset.

14. What are the two things that are the mind of the flesh?

15. What is the sole purpose of the mind?

16. The battle between the _____ and the _____ rages because the flesh doesn't want you to submit to the Spirit of Christ.

CHAPTER 3 QUESTIONS
UNDERSTANDING THE PROPHETIC

We also have the prophetic message as something completely reliable, and you will do well to pay attention to it, as to a light shining in a dark place, until the day dawns and the morning star rises in your hearts. **2 Peter 1:19**

KEY TERMS

Realm - A range or field of control, power, or other concentration of mastery and or authority

Power - legal or official authority, capacity, or right

The prophetic is not some mystical, spooky place that is only reserved for a select few. In fact, it is the greatest establishment in the earth because it causes the invisible to become visible. God wants everyone to have knowledge about how the prophetic functions, operates, speaks and manifests. The prophetic is the power source God used to create the world and every living thing he placed in it.

1. Who interprets the mind of God to his people?

2. What does prophecy give you and the prophetic?

3. What are the effects of the prophetic being silenced in the church?

4. The prophetic is the power of the _____ and _____ coming together to invade the earth.

5. What is the prophetic the greatest establishment on the earth?

6. God wants everyone to have knowledge about how the prophetic _____, _____, _____, and _____.

7. Operating prophetic realms can be likened unto having "_____" abilities.

8. Identify the prophetic resources in the diagram below:

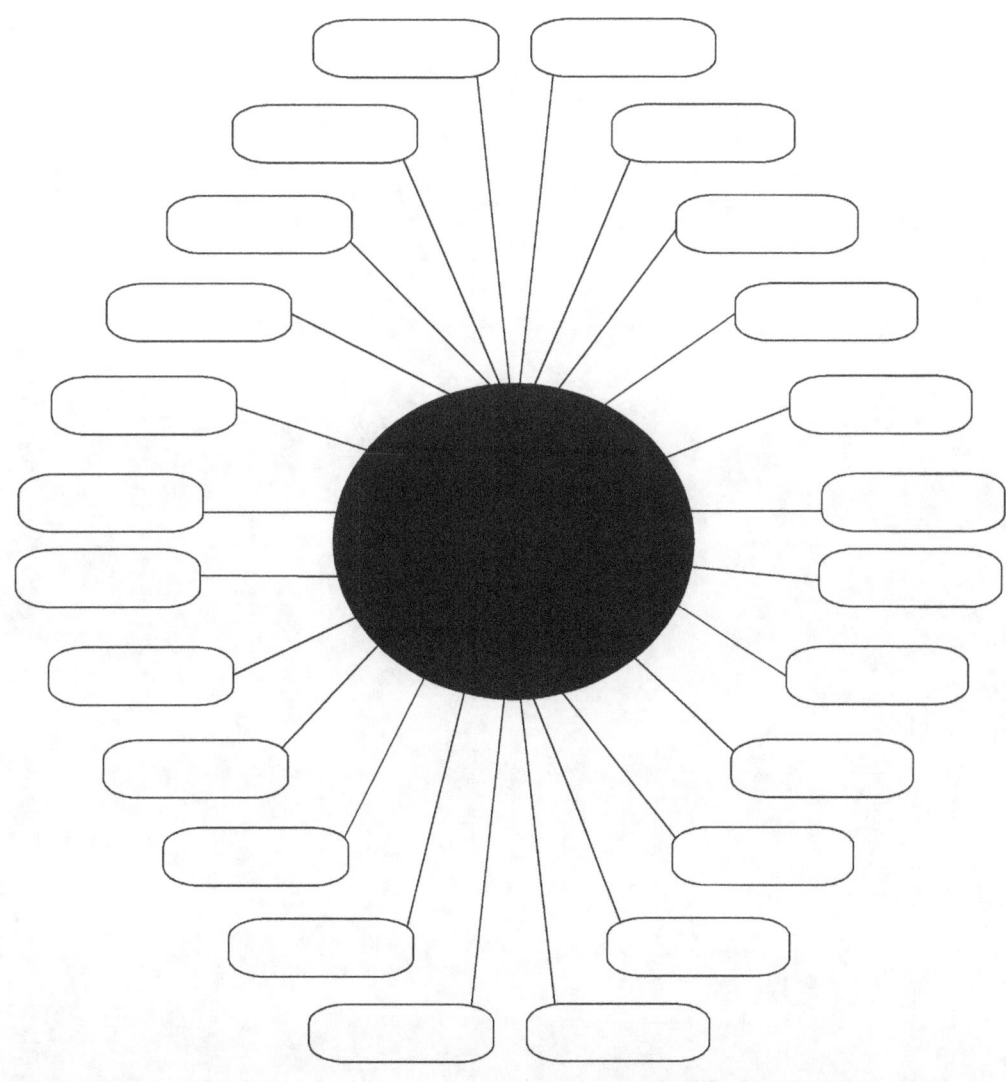

9. What is the purpose of the fivefold ministry?

10. God is calling us forth to merge our mantles and work together as _____ _____ with _____ _____ to demonstrate the power of his kingdom and to become his hands extended in the earth.

CHAPTER 4 QUESTIONS
CULTIVATING A PROPHETIC MINDSET

For as a man thinks in his heart so is he, not as he thinks in his head.

Proverbs 23:7 Amplified

KEY TERMS

Cultivation - knowing that something exists or is happening

Mindset - a mental attitude or inclination, a fixed state of mind

In order to benefit from the prophetic, you must be willing to change the way you think and open your heart and mind to receive truth about this powerful supernatural realm. The heart is the cultivating ground of change however; the mind where all decisions are made. A prerequisite to having a prophetic mindset is tilling the soil of your mind. Tilling the soil of the mind involves picking, plucking and plowing up religious thoughts that may have caused you to be in a dry or even barren place in your salvation.

1. Why is the heart the cultivating ground for change?

2. Explain the formula: The Holy Spirit + The Word of God = New Light?

3. What two things are included in the process of renewing your mind?

a.

b.

4. What is a prerequisite to having a prophetic mindset?

5. What are the five keys to cultivate a prophetic mindset?

      a) _____

      b) _____

      c) _____

      d) _____

      e) _____

6. If you receive the Word of God in your _____ and not just into your _____, you will produce all of the fruit of the spirit.

7. Too often, we focus on the _____ _____ instead of the _____ _____.

8. What is one of the greatest pleasures of the father?

9. Explain how life in the spirit comes.

10. What tool connects you to God's way of thinking?

CHAPTER 5 QUESTIONS
A HIGHER WAY OF THINKING

For as the heavens are higher than the earth, so are my ways higher than your ways, and my thoughts than your thoughts. **Isaiah 55:9 ESV**

KEY TERMS

Perspective - The capacity to view things in their true relations or relative importance

Dispensation - Administration

Shifting into a higher way of thinking requires you to not only be transformed in your mind, but for you to study and read the word and have a consistent prayer life. A renewed mind is the precursor to lead you to a higher and better way of thinking by way of the Spirit, so that you can be powerful and defeat the enemy. Higher thoughts of the spirit mean that you will begin to walk in the perfect will of God.

1. List four things that you are required to do in order to shift into a higher way of thinking:

    a) _____

    b) _____

    c) _____

    d) _____

2. _____ has the privilege to get _____ by way of the _____.

3. **True or False (circle one)**
   Spiritual blessings and finances come as a result of spending time with the Lord.

4. How is the Holy Spirit like our GPS system?

5. A _____ _____ is the precursor to lead you to a higher and better way of thinking by way of the Spirit, so that you can be powerful and defeat the enemy.

6. _____ _____ which leads to reasoning and intellectualization, is a form of pride.

7. What are the three things that free us from bondage?

   a) _____

   b) _____

   c) _____

8. **True or False (circle one)**
   The term familiar spirits is derived from generation spirit that supplied a family with its supernatural knowledge, worldly possessions, success, and spiritual wisdom.

9. We are living in an hour where we can't afford to _____ to, or be _____ by, any sound other than the Spirit of God. _____ relate to what is seen in the earth realm and _____ abides in the realm that is unseen.

10. **True or False (circle one)**
    God wants us to live victoriously on earth.

11. The only reason we contend with problems in the earth is because we don't have a _____ _____.

12. What is short-term memory?

13. What is long-term memory?

14. Why do we think negative thoughts?

CHAPTER 6 QUESTIONS
THE PROPHETIC SPIRIT

Now the Word of the LORD came to me saying, Before I formed you in the womb I knew you, And before you were born I consecrated you; I have appointed you a prophet to the nations." **Jeremiah 1:4-5 ESV**

KEY TERMS

Portal - An egress for traversing back and forth and for transporting products sent between two locations. Spiritually, that would be between two worlds

Supernatural - That which operates and controls our natural world from the spiritual world above our own

The spirit of every living creature comes from God. You can change the outward appearance of something, but it won't change the spirit of it. The spirit of a man is the spirit of a man. Even if you dress him like a woman, the spirit of the man is still present. As you grow prophetically, you will begin to notice a new awareness of spiritual and supernatural things developing in your life. Just like any process in life, there are stages of development which prepare you to fully understand and exercise the power contained within the prophetic spirit.

1. What are prophetic realms?

2. God _____ and _____ us with everything we need to operate as powerful prophetic agents.

3. **True or False (circle one)**
   Prophetic realms are the areas of concentration or mastery where God gives you dominion and rulership.

4. What happens when you begin to grow prophetically?

5. The _____ or _____ stage is where you begin to see your life take on a new perspective.

6. Prophets and prophetic types receive communications like: _____, _____, _____, by what they see in the spirit or what they hear by the spirit.

7. When God speaks you will get _____ and _____ to correspond with what he has said.

8. **True or False (circle one)**
Prophetic gifts are confined to the Holy Spirit's manifestations.

9. The prophet can _____ at will, the _____ _____ is mostly restricted to prophesying by the unction of the Holy Spirit.

10. **True or False (circle one)**
All prophetic gifts are officers, but all officers have prophetic gifts.

11. Define the essence of a prophet?

12. The occult realms deal with the following:

    P_____

    C_____

    S_____

    N_____

    S_____

13. What do psychics forecast? _____ _____

14. _____ sets things in motion in the spirit realm because God desires for something to be accomplished here on earth.

15. **True or False (circle one)**
    There is a voice within the voice of prophesy that speaks to all of creation to cause it to hear and respond when God speaks.

CHAPTER 7 QUESTIONS
THE MIND OF PROPHECY

Follow after charity, and desire spiritual gifts, but rather that ye may prophesy.

I Corinthians 14:1 KJV

KEY TERMS

Revelatory - That which emanates from, or emerges as, a revelation of God's truth as found in His Word

Revelation - The disclosed Word of God

Prophecy is one of the most potent resources of the prophetic and it comes from the predictive spheres. The predictive spheres give you the ability to enter into the spirit realm and get foreknowledge on your circumstance and say to it what God says. Prophecy is an inspired communication from God. When you prophesy you are speaking forth the revealed mind of God.

1. What is the distinction between prophetic and prophecy?

2. What is the primary purpose for prophecy?

3. What is the function of the prophecy?

4. What is prophetic accuracy?

5. Prophecy is the gift of the _____; and in order for the utterance to occur, _____ must be present.

6. The bible says that we prophesy according to the measure of our faith. Please expound on this in your own words.

7. Where there is faith _____ and _____ can't exist.

8. Why is it important to operate in the realm of faith?

9. When the prophetic word is released, where does it meet you?

10. What are the opponents of prophecy? What must be done to remove those limitations.

CHAPTER 8 QUESTIONS
PROPHETIC PRAYER

Jesus answered and said unto them, Verily I say unto you, If ye have faith, and doubt not, ye shall not only do this [which is done] to the fig tree, but also if ye shall say unto this mountain, Be thou removed, and be thou cast into the sea; it shall be done. And all things, whatsoever ye shall ask in prayer, believing, ye shall receive. ***Matthew 21:21-22 KJV***

KEY TERMS

Authority - the power to give orders or make decisions: the power or right to direct or control someone or something

Sphere - an arena or region of influence or activity that is more figurative than literal. A Word for the immaterial territories of influence and control embedded in creation

Heaven is constantly invading the earth and the most common means is through prophetic prayer. Prophetic prayer is conducted by the prophet or prophetic types with the express purpose of compelling the manifestation of a prophecy. It always has intercessory overtones and exhibits strong authoritative commands to spiritual forces others usually cannot see. They require relentless faith and are strategic and tactical in nature.

1. Define the word sphere.

2. Prophetic prayer is conducted by the _____ or _____ _____ with the express purpose of compelling the manifestation of a prophecy.

3. What takes place when we pray prophetically?

4. Why is the Lord's Prayer considered a Prophetic Prayer?

5. _____ gives you access into the prophetic spheres and whenever you pray prophetic prayers, you are bringing God thoughts into your now.

6. **True or False (circle one)**
   When we pray prophetically we are praying the world's agenda.

7. A _____ that is filled with faith will change the trajectory of your prophetic prayers.

8. **True or False (circle one)**
   In prayer God downloads strategies and the blueprints for what he wants to accomplish.

9. What are the four P's that are in the Lord's Prayer?

   a. _____

   b. _____

   c. _____

   d. _____ _____

10. When you pray prophetically, you _____ in that place as God's _____ with full _____ to speak forth his word into the earth.

Answer Key for Chapter 1

1. It is at enmity against God. It opposes God.

2. Carnal mind, spiritual mind

3. The unconscious mind.

4. God desires for believers to live in abundance and not be limited in any way.

5. Focus, eventually

6. The human mind is limited to the earth realm.

7. The "sixth sense" gives people the ability to perceive the unseen world.

8. The unconscious mind stores deep seated emotions that have been programmed in us since birth. It is likened to a vault where memories have been repressed.

9. The core of our thinking and belief system.

10. The conscious mind directs your ability to focus.

11. Limitation

12. A prophetic attitude will always give you an advantage in your career, business, relationships, at home, and all things pertaining your very existence, for it is an elevated way of reflecting and subsisting. Having an attitude of such permits you to always be on top.

Answer Key for Chapter 2

1. You must be transformed by the renewing of your mind. Romans 12:2

2. Thinks, acts

3. Disobedience blocks transformation because it causes a spiritual separation between you and God.

4. Heavens, earth

5. When the mind is transformed your very character and nature takes on a new identity.

6. Wrestle

7. Block, prophetic, mind of the flesh

8. Eden symbolizes a rich and fertile place of unbroken fellowship.

9. Change your thoughts and you change your world.

10. Thoughts that come from a lower world and not the mind of God.

11. Disobedience

12. Predestined, designed

13. Carnal, fleshly

14. The mind of the flesh-which largely deals with the cravings and desires of what we want and not what God desires, is what we were taught and trained to focus on and believe in, it is a mind of reason and sense.

15. The sole purpose of the mind of the flesh leads you to death and opposes whatever God stands for.

16. Flesh, spirit

Answer Key for Chapter 3

1. It is the ministry voice that interprets the mind of God to his people.

2. The prophecy gives you information. The prophetic tears down, establishes, builds, charges, ignites, navigates, re-directs and steers.

3. When the prophetic is silenced it will be difficult to hear from God because the prophetic offers strategies and solutions.

4. Prophetic, prophet's mantle

5. The prophetic is not some mystical, spooky place that is only reserved for a select few. It is fact, the greatest establishment in the earth because it causes the invisible to become visible.

6. Functions, operates, speaks, manifests

7. Superhero

8. Visions, discernment, words of wisdom, words of knowledge, discerning of spirits, counsel & might, psalmists, faith, love, seraphim, watchers, cherubim, holy ones, ministering spirits, archangels, angels, seers, prophets, apostles, spiritual warfare, intercession, prayer, miracles, dreams

9. The fivefold was given to build and equip the Body by utilizing all five officers. We may all have different gifts, classifications, spheres of influence and measures of rule but it is important to remember they have been given for one purpose and that is to fortify the kingdom.

10. Governmental forces, spiritual intelligence

Answer Key for Chapter 4

1. The heart houses your mind, will and emotions, and it holds the greatest influence to every decision in life.

2. The Spirit represents the water which is the word of God. The Word of God must go into your mind so that new seeds of God's thoughts can grow and so that light can be produced in your life.

3. Involves uprooting old thoughts and replacing them with new thoughts.

4. Tilling the soil of your mind. Tilling the soil of the mind involves picking, plucking, plowing up religious thoughts that may have caused you to be in a dry or even a barren place in your salvation.

5. Prayer, Transformation of the Mind, death, Studying the word of God, Christ formed in you

6. Spirit, life

7. Doing in love, the dying in love

8. One of the greatest pleasures of the Father is when He sees us take in the seed and allow the water and light to nurture it so that we can grow and bear fruit.

9. Self-denial, the more you die to your selfish ways the more you will walk in the life of the spirit.

10. Prayer connects you to God's way of thinking. It is the tool that allows us to communicate with God to get heaven to respond on our behalf.

Answer Key for Chapter 5

1. a. be transformed in your mind b. study the word c. read the word d. have a consistent prayer life

2. Everyone; revelation; spirit

3. True

4. Because it leads us directly into the high places of God, where his revelatory thoughts reside

5. Renewed mind

6. Carnal thinking

7. 3 things: live a spirit filled life, have a renewed mind and have spiritual intelligence (pnuema)

8. True

9. Listen, influenced

10. True

11. Is when an electro chemical occurrence tales place in the brain, that takes a picture but it doesn't become fixed or locked

12. Reinforces things by meditation and repetition causing it to be locked into your consciousness (awareness)

13. Is directly connected to the negative sound that "fell out" of heaven when Satan got kicked out with a third of the angels. Basically, when you sit and dwell in negative sounds, they will cultivate negative seed-thoughts making it difficult to receive truth

14. Supernatural Realm

Answer Key for Chapter 6

1. Prophetic realms are the areas of concentration or mastery where God gives you dominion and ruler ship to operate in authority to utilize your spiritual and supernatural tools.

2. Created; equipped

3. True

4. You will begin to notice a new awareness of spiritual and supernatural things developing in your life

5. Awareness; awakening

6. Dreams; visions; prophecies

7. Pictures; images

8. True

9. Prophesy, prophetic gift

10. False

11. A person who has been given license to go in and out of the spiritual spheres and speak forth which is seen and heard in terrains of heaven. A mouthpiece

12. Psychics, clairvoyants, spiritists, necromancers, soothsayers

13. Satan's mind

14. Prophesying

15. True

Answer Key for Chapter 7

1. The prophetic is the portal that opens the door to prophecy

2. The primary purpose for prophecy is to uncover and unveil, to make (previously unknown information) known to others.

3. Prophecy's function is to transfer the thought of God through the voice of man; to interject God's will through a series of events that He orchestrates for the good of man.

4. Prophetic Accuracy defines the prophet's skill in accurately delivering the Word of the Lord.

5. Spirit; faith

6. The extent of what we are able to receive prophetically is determined upon the extent of our faith. The greater faith we have, the greater the ability to receive the prophetic word and deliver it accordingly.

7. Doubt; fear

8. When you operate in the realm of faith you can access the mind of God.

9. The prophetic word meets you at your place of faith. In order to remove doubt, you must believe that God is who he says he is and exercise your faith muscles. Take him at his word.

10. Doubt and Fear

Answer Key for Chapter 8

1. An arena or region of influence or activity that is more figurative than literal. A word for the immaterial territories of influence and control embedded in creation.

2. Prophet; prophetic types

3. We pray the Kingdom's agenda We pray from heaven's perspective and not Earth's, declaring out of the predictive sphere what will happen at the appointed time.

4. It is a prophetic prayer because activates the mind and will of God to the earth

5. Faith

6. False

7. Prayer

8. True

9. Praise, petition, penitence, prophetic proclamation

10. Stand, spokesperson, authority, speak forth

NOTES

NOTES

NOTES

NOTES

NOTES

NOTES

Bibliography

Merriam-Webster.com. 2011. **http://www.merriam-webster.com**

The Human Mind – How Does It All Work?" Mindset Habits. 20 May 2010. Web.

Price, Paula A. The Prophet's Dictionary: The Ultimate Guide to Supernatural Wisdom. 2006

Blue Letter Bible. Web. 13 Aug. 2013

Sparks, T. A. "What Prophetic Ministry Is." Prophetic Ministry: A Classic Study of the Nature of a Prophet. 2. Print

www.ingramcontent.com/pod-product-compliance
Lightning Source LLC
Chambersburg PA
CBHW060520300426

44112CB00017B/2739